When
HOPE
Is Not Enough

A 30-Year Journey of Faith & Community

Written and Compiled
by Lynn Bohart

VISIONHOUSE

Published by Pacelli Publishing
Bellevue, Washington

When Hope Is Not Enough:
A 30-Year Journey of Faith & Community

Published by Pacelli Publishing
9905 Lake Washington Blvd. NE, #D-103
Bellevue, Washington 98004
PacelliPublishing.com

Printed in the United States of America

Formatting, editing, and cover design: Pacelli Publishing

Cover photo: Stephanie Dyane, StephanieDyane.com

ISBN-10: 1-933750-68-5
ISBN-13: 978-1-933750-68-2

ACKNOWLEDGEMENTS

The making of Vision House has relied on the dedication and generosity of thousands of volunteers, donors, and staff members. It has been a labor of love for all who have touched this amazing program since its beginning in 1990.

This book is meant to give a shout-out to everyone who played a role in the founding, expansion, and success of Vision House. We are especially indebted, however, to the following people who traveled this journey together and helped to bring the Vision House story to life by sharing their fondest memories.

Contributors: Jay and Diana Wallace, Ted and Becky Almquist, Kurt Campbell, Craig Campbell, Bob and Roberta Sime, Sylvia Holden, Mike Young, Tim Berg.

Staff: Melissa Gehrig, Executive Director; Venetia Vango, Development Manager

Founders: John and Susan Camerer

CONTENTS

INTRODUCTION

Just imagine.

You are a young woman, forced to flee an abusive husband who has threatened your life, only to find yourself living on the streets. Your personal security is still a day-by-day struggle—but not from your spouse. No. Now, you struggle to stay safe from drug dealers. Pimps. And people who will do anything to take advantage of you or steal what little you have.

Each day you must withstand the gnawing pangs of hunger. The anxiety of not knowing where you will sleep when the streets become dark. You must even withstand the undignified lack of bathroom facilities and clean clothes.

And, you're doing this all while holding the hand of your four-year-old daughter.

At night, you dream of a better life, and each day you hope your situation will change. After all, life isn't supposed to be like this. Not in America.

You do everything you can to turn things around. You apply for government assistance. You seek out shelters and visit clothing banks and food pantries.

And yet, your hope dwindles as days stretch into weeks, and weeks into months, and still you live on the streets.

How is a young mother supposed to rise above these circumstances when life seems stacked against her? What choices does she have?

There is an answer. And it's Vision House.

Vision House is a nonprofit organization that brings parents who have custody of their children off the streets and into safe and secure transitional housing. Vision House was the breakthrough idea of founders John and Susan Camerer. Inspired by their Christian faith and belief in God's grace, they made a commitment to provide a place where women and men would be given the support and guidance they needed to get back on their feet, while protecting their children.

"I find it interesting," says Susan, "that when God truly calls us to something bigger than ourselves, He doesn't lay out all of the details or steps that it is going to take to move forward."

Through a tremendous amount of trial and error, unwavering dedication, and a coming together of like-minded individuals and companies, Vision House has become a beacon of hope for hundreds of women, men, and children who find themselves homeless and alone.

After 30 years and scores of success stories, Vision House is celebrating what it means to dig deep into a problem, develop a successful model, and build loving collaborations. This foundation makes a real difference in the lives of people who have fallen through the cracks of a broken system and lost hope in the American dream.

Join us through the following pages of this commemorative book as we share their 30-year commitment. The journey was not always easy, nor was the path always straight. But Vision House has benefitted from the magic of inspiration, the love of God, and the dedication of many hard-working staff, volunteers, and donors focused solely on restoring a feeling of hope, safety, and dignity to the people who needed them.

When hope is not enough to help a lost soul rise above their circumstances, it takes a program like Vision House to serve as the bridge to a new life.

This is a story of when good was done. Lives were changed. And faith prevailed.

> *"For I know the plans I have for you," declares the Lord,*
> *"plans to prosper you and not to harm you,*
> *plans to give you a hope and a future."*
> **—Jeremiah 29:11**

1

A LEAP OF FAITH

"God calls you to the place where your deep gladness and the world's deep hunger meet."
—Frederick Buechner

It's funny sometimes how stories begin; each one begins differently. Whether it opens with "Once upon a time…" or "In a galaxy far, far away…," the genesis of a story is unique. And, from beginning to end, each path the story takes will be unique as well.

Writers will tell you that it's the characters and the players *in* the story that determine whether it will end with success or failure. This is because the outcome depends on the players' commitment to the result. Their dedication. Their resourcefulness and their willingness to change and grow as the story progresses.

Vision House has such a story.

After 30 years of overcoming a variety of obstacles and adversity, the path Vision House took brought it to where it is today — a highly successful agency that helps those experiencing homelessness get back on their feet. That journey brought Vision House to a place where it is now filled with light and promise. Not just for the people they serve, but for the communities they serve and the donors and volunteers who keep the story going.

How it began–the calling

John & Susan Camerer

This story begins with a quiet night at home.

There was nothing unusual about that night. The room didn't shake. There were no booming voices or bright lights. But it was a night that would dramatically change the lives of John and Susan Camerer forever.

The year was 1989.

It was a beautiful spring night, and John and Susan had just tucked their infant son, Brandon, into bed for the night. Wishing for a little alone time, they retired to the den to watch some TV and turned on a made-for-television movie called *God Bless the Child.*

The story that unfolded was that of a single mom and her young daughter. They were about to lose their home because their property was being redeveloped into market-rate condominiums, which the young mother couldn't afford on a housekeeper's salary.

Unable to find another apartment, she was forced to enter the public shelter system with her daughter, moving from shelter to shelter when their allotted time was up. Eventually, the daughter developed lead poisoning from the rundown buildings, and the mother was told that if she didn't remove her child from the exposure to lead, it could result in irreparable brain damage.

Mom was at the end of her rope and felt she had only two options: give up her child to the State or move out of the shelters and onto the street.

Neither choice was a good one.

The movie ended with this distraught and heartbroken mother making the ultimate sacrifice; she allowed Child Protective Services to take her daughter in order to keep the girl safe and healthy.

John and Susan were struck by many things that night. The unfairness of what happened to this young woman. The fact she was a good mother; she was kind and loving toward her daughter. The fact that she had no family and no support system to help in her time of need. And, the fact that it takes more than love to raise a healthy child.

They went to bed heartbroken at the thought this might truly be happening to families in their own community. As they contemplated the enormity of it all, the thought of their own son and their vulnerability as young parents was foremost in their minds.

As Susan says, "We were new parents ourselves and contemplated how it would feel to have our family torn apart — to lose a child."

So, the couple went to bed asking, "God, if this story could ever really happen to a family, will you allow us to do something about it?"

The foundation

"Yet you, LORD, are our Father. We are the clay,
you are the potter; we are all the work of your hand."
—Isaiah 64:8

The foundation of why John and Susan Camerer decided to lend their time and talent to helping the homeless wasn't just in response to the movie they had watched; it is far more fundamental than that. In fact, although their early lives were diametrically opposed to one another, those years prepared each of them for the champions they would eventually become. And God had a hand in that.

Susan grew up in a loving and secure home, the third of four girls in the family. Her mom and dad ran a small auto repair shop from their five-acre farm on the outskirts of Tacoma. Although busy, her parents were always available to their daughters. And the doors were open to others in need as well.

In fact, it was never a surprise for the girls to come downstairs for breakfast and find a kitchen table full of family, friends, and perhaps a repair customer or two enjoying coffee and the latest community news and events. Breakfast was often eaten standing up, because there was no room for everyone to sit down.

"The smell of coffee, sound of laughter, and conversation filled our home with love and warmth," Susan remembers.

She refers to her childhood home as "Metamorphosis House," because rooms were often added, remodeled, or repurposed to accommodate a weary traveler, a returning daughter, a sick friend, a lonely child, or a foreign exchange student. All who entered the home were welcome.

This forged Susan into the woman she is today.

John, on the other hand, grew up in an often violent and dysfunctional home with alcoholic parents.

"Perhaps I connect with the need for someone to provide a hand up to those in need," John says. "And so, I became that person."

But John will tell you that his journey was a long and tortuous one.

John grew up in South Seattle as the youngest of four children. Since his two sisters were older, he spent most of his childhood with only his older brother in the home. For a significant part of John's life, family values weren't a priority, and the boys had little supervision.

At an early age, John began to imitate the behavior he observed in his parents — smoking, drinking, and later, drugs. Although his parents required that they attend a local church, the requirement was difficult to enforce because they often had hangovers on Sunday mornings. The fact that his parents didn't attend church sent the message to John that it really wasn't that important.

So, growing up, John didn't give much thought to God or religion. However, as Susan says, "Even though we may not be aware of God's purpose for our life, or notice His work around us, it doesn't mean that HE isn't in pursuit of a relationship with us." John would eventually discover that to be true.

Besides the heavy drinking, John's father was abusive toward his mother. After one particularly frightful experience, John sought refuge with some neighbors.

Bill and Jean Phelan lived next door. Bill was the vice principal and a football coach at an inner-city high school and had a son about John's age. While Bill tended to John's mom that night, his wife Jean stayed with John and assured him he was safe. Later, as he rested, he noticed something unusual about Bill and Jean's home—it was quiet . . . peaceful. He felt secure for the first time in his young life as he drifted off to sleep in silence. Over the coming years, the Phelan home would become a haven for John, and Bill would become a mentor and a friend.

But as is true for many of us, John's life lessons came hard. Although a talented athlete, he continued to use drugs and alcohol throughout high school and into college. John was able to compartmentalize his alcohol and drug use, however, so that he could play sports and attend college. Unfortunately, this led him to a life of lies and an unhealthy lifestyle.

But God had better plans for John.

Bill Phelan became a surrogate father, often attending John's high school games, charting his successes, and giving him guidance. John's relationship with Bill and Jean during that time has given John the strong conviction that mentors—safe, caring adults, teachers, coaches and neighbors who invest in the lives of troubled kids—can have a significant impact on a child's life.

According to studies:

- The single best predictor of children becoming either perpetrators or victims of domestic violence later in life is whether or not they grow up in a home where there is domestic violence.[i]

- Boys who witness domestic violence are twice as likely to abuse their own partners and children when they become adults.[ii]

- Children who were exposed to violence in the home are 15 times more likely to be physically and/or sexually assaulted than the national average.[iii]

Domestic violence expert, Nancy Murphy, Ph.D., says that "a sympathetic, caring adult" is the single most important element to make a difference in the life of a child who has witnessed domestic violence in the home. What a simple solution to such a complex issue!

For John, Bill was that sympathetic, caring adult. If you talk to Bill, however, he will shrug off the role he played in John's life as nothing spectacular or heroic.

"I was just a friend and a neighbor," he responds.

John eventually began attending Pacific Lutheran University (PLU) in Tacoma. He was still struggling with alcohol and drugs and suffered a big emotional blow—he lost the love of a girl he cared for deeply. This stopped him dead in his tracks, forcing him to question his spirituality and the meaning of life. He reached out to some of the Christian athletes at PLU, asking them questions about their faith.

One of John's high school friends, Garth Warren, who played football at PLU, began to spend time with John, explaining what Christianity was all about. He changed John's perception of Christians as being weak and not having any fun. His friend shared God's blessing and the joy one can have living for Christ.

John was impacted by this and went home one night and got on his knees and repented of his sins, asking Jesus to take control of his life. He recalls an immediate transformation. Drugs were no longer an issue, and he would cringe at the sound of profanity. His friend introduced him to a good church, and along with a few other athletes, he helped to lead a Bible study.

Eventually, John's parents worked hard to attain sobriety and recommitted their marriage and life to Jesus Christ.

John graduated from Pacific Lutheran University with a bachelor's degree in Crime in Society Sociology and a minor degree in Organizational Communication. His background and previous illegal drug use kept him from becoming a police officer, but he began a career at Rap House Work Release in Tacoma. Eventually, he transferred to the Washington Corrections Center in Shelton, then King County Juvenile Detention Center, and later worked as a corrections counselor with Snohomish County Corrections.

And, this is where our story begins.

The beginning

Sometimes in life things just seem meant to be, as if God has placed a hand on our backs to move us in the right direction.

In this case, John was working at Snohomish County Corrections, and Susan was a small business owner. They were also new parents. Neither of them needed another job or more to do. And yet, after that movie about the young mother losing her home and then her daughter, they couldn't shrug off the feeling that they were being called to a greater purpose—one that would do more than test their mettle—it would test their faith.

> *"For we are God's handiwork, created in Christ Jesus to do good works, which God prepared in advance for us to do."*
> **—Ephesians 2:10**

After some serious soul-searching, deep discussions, and a flurry of phone calls, John and Susan decided to act. They would play a role in helping the homeless find the traction they needed to get back on their feet.

John already had a deep understanding about how hard it was to find housing with integrated support services, especially for those exiting the prison system or adults in recovery from drug and alcohol addiction. Every day in his office at the corrections department, John would counsel inmates who had sincere intentions of changing the direction of their lives. Their incarceration had given them some time to think, sober up, and prepare to stop abusing illegal drugs and alcohol. These inmates vowed there would be no more criminal activity and that they were transformed.

However, John knew that once he signed the papers for their release, and they returned to their old environment, their friends and family members would influence them again. This made the chances of recidivism high.

John had always believed that if these men just had a healthy place to go, and an environment with a mentor to guide them, they would have a chance to succeed. They could experience a different way to live, develop new life skills, and receive counseling and support. He was convinced that if these men's physical needs could be met, then he would have the opportunity to show Christ's love for them and make a lasting difference in their lives.

Because John was already familiar with the needs of a men's population, he and Susan decided to begin by developing a single men's program.

But creating a full-fledged nonprofit organization from scratch is no small feat. John took the lead and stumbled through the process, first obtaining Washington State nonprofit status and then assembling a board, a mission statement, and a set of bylaws to apply to the federal government for tax exempt status.

"Our goal was to develop a service model of transitional housing that would address the inequities in education, employment, social services and health care affecting the homeless," says John.

In other words, not a quick fix.

Research points to many reasons that someone experiences homelessness in the first place. Loss of a job. Overwhelming healthcare costs. Conflict with parents. An abusive spouse. Addiction. Foreclosure on a home. And the lack of skills to manage their finances, advocate for themselves, and/or train for a new job.

So, any program designed to get people back on their feet had to be both diverse and inclusive.

"Our dream was to develop a place of refuge and recovery, where residents could learn everyday skills and not a place to just go for a handout," says Susan.

John's experience with the DOC came in very handy. It gave him the ability to develop a structured case management program where accountability was an important part of the client's recovery, facilitating their return to mainstream society. The model would require residents to pay a minimal amount of rent (30 percent of their income, usually about $100) to cover utilities and maintenance of the home.

"The rent structure has always been an important part of the Vision House program," says John. This models real-life budgeting.

The goal was to have clients sign a lease, so that Vision House would serve as their landlord. This would give them a rental history. When clients were ready to move to permanent housing, Vision House could then provide them with a positive referral. For a population that has poor credit and/or has been evicted multiple times, a rental history and positive referral would be critical to their success.

But supportive skills are also necessary to help someone maintain their independence. John focused on this aspect of the program, developing a comprehensive case management system, which would include a process to assess each client's situation, develop a plan forward, facilitate that plan, evaluate progress, and then advocate for other necessary services to meet the individual's needs. This would give the men the best chance at making positive changes in their lives.

John and Susan began to put together a plan for what they hoped to accomplish. In June of 1990, John met with Mike Smith, the Missions Pastor at Highlands Community Church in Renton, to discuss Vision House ministry and what role the church could play.

"Mike and I were mapping out the Vision House ministry, when I asked him whether Vision House could be a ministry of Highlands. He stopped and looked right at me and said, 'NO, you don't want to limit yourselves to one church or one community.'"

Pastor Mike went on to say that Vision House had the potential to be much bigger than just the Highlands area. It could represent the whole body of Christ and not one denomination.

"I was looking for security," says John, "and thought about fitting under an established ministry. But Mike saw the bigger picture and vision."

A few months later, John and Susan opened their first home for men in recovery. But they needed $500 for liability insurance. They went to Pastor Mike and asked if they could borrow this amount and pay him back when the men paid rent and some donations came in.

Pastor Mike was able to secure the funds from the church, and the Camerers never looked back. A few months later, John presented a repayment check to Mike, who merely smiled and said, "It was a gift."

"We need more Mike Smiths in the world to encourage, guide, and mentor young men with vision," John says.

2

WHEN YOU KNOW IT'S GO TIME

It seemed logical to begin their program with a single-family home. The couple found a willing landlord to rent them one and wrote a personal check for $800 to cover the deposit and first month's rent. This was the moment of truth, and their excitement grew as they anticipated starting the program with men experiencing homelessness.

It wasn't long, however, before they became aware of a better deal.

The U.S. Department of Housing and Urban Development (HUD) offered five-year leases for only $1 a year for abandoned homes. That was a price they couldn't beat. Unfortunately, many of the HUD homes required expensive repairs or remodeling using money they didn't have.

Suddenly, the perfect solution wasn't so perfect anymore. What could they do?

"For us, it wasn't clear at all how to start a ministry, develop a successful program, raise money, or build homes and apartments," Susan remembers. "But we knew that if we just followed God's lead and searched out where He was working, things would fall into place."

Fortunately, the Camerers were strong in faith. As they faced this first hurdle and asked God how to proceed, they knew in their hearts they were on the right path. They also knew they would need a small miracle to get started.

"We would often just stop and pray," says Susan. "and small miracles would happen."

And sure enough, their prayers were answered. A home that was only a year old and in great condition became available through HUD. They thanked God and paid their $1 per year lease. On November 12, 1990, they opened their first transitional housing unit for men recovering from drug and alcohol addiction.

Four men moved into the facility and Vision House became official. John and a volunteer met with the men as needed to help them with their journey toward sobriety. They would also offer weekly recovery Bible studies and meet one-on-one with the men to meet individual needs.

John remembers one of them saying that he had never felt more respected, loved, and cared for in his life. He told John, "This is the beginning of a new life for me."

John felt enormously humbled and appreciated the encouragement. But he also knew that one out five men would return to their former substance abuse within a year. In fact, in the mandatory house meeting they held once a week, John would often remind the men that the statistics were not on their side. For that reason, he encouraged them to fight for their sobriety as if it was a life or death struggle. "Because," he said, "it was."

Bolstered by their early success, John and Susan opened their second home in Maple Valley in 1991. During that first year of ministry, Vision House served 24 men in recovery, giving them a second chance at a new life.

When God gives you lemons, make lemonade

As anyone in the nonprofit world knows, managing a startup isn't easy. There are many of challenges, obstacles, and yes, failures along the way. This is often referred to as "growing pains." And painful it can be.

Vision House was no different.

In 1993, John and Susan opened their third home, this time for single women recovering from drug and alcohol addiction, and experiencing homelessness. Everyone was excited to provide the women a stable, warm home for Christmas.

Third home – began as a facility for women
recovering from substance abuse.

While the staff and volunteers at Vision House felt blessed that they could give women experiencing homelessness a safe place to stay during the holidays, they didn't consider what a difficult time the holidays can be for some people. Psychologists say that the holidays are hard for many, particularly those who feel broken and discarded by their loved ones.

"It's especially true for people in recovery," says Susan. "They remember better times, lost relationships, abuse, and they grieve about how things could have been. They long for healed relationships."

During those early days, the women under Vision House's care struggled. There were arguments and fighting in the home, along with two suicide attempts.

"We had difficulty finding volunteers at that time," John reports. "And frankly, the program felt unstable."

But the couple persevered until one of the women relapsed and began to drink again and was asked to leave. Fearful she may return and cause harm to someone, they encouraged the other women to find someplace else to stay that night. This turned out to be good advice. The woman in question did return and took a crowbar to the windows and much of the interior of the home.

"Our hearts were broken," Susan laments. "We wondered how someone we were called to minister to could become so violent and destructive."

This incident brought into stark focus the potential downside to what they were doing. John and Susan became painfully aware that a single women's program required more intensive case management and service support than they could provide with just a small team of volunteers.

So, in 1993, they made a difficult decision and shut down the single women's program.

Susan remembers sitting on a blanket in the front yard holding their newborn son, Austin, while John boarded up the home. It was Father's Day, and they both felt a sense of defeat. That was a low point for the young couple, and not surprisingly, they questioned their calling.

"But looking back, I realized the single women's program wasn't a mistake," Susan says. "I believe that God allows us to fail. We learn, we grow, we dust ourselves off and become better and stronger from what we learned."

There was a bright spot to this failure. With a little elbow grease, they cleaned up the home and reopened it as a home for men in recovery. And, although temporarily delayed, their initial desire to serve women experiencing homelessness who had custody of children and needed a safe place to live never waned.

God's messengers

Immediately upon meeting John and Susan Camerer, you'll notice their lust for life, their enthusiasm to make a difference in the world, and their unlimited faith in God's grace and provision. You only need to talk with them for a short time to be inspired by their positive attitudes and true love for people and their stories, including the hurting and the homeless. With God at their backs, they continued their journey, "realizing that God doesn't call us to do something and then not provide what is needed to fulfill that calling," says Susan. "We just needed to trust Him."

One of Susan's favorite quotes by Mother Theresa is, "God does not demand that I be successful. God demands that I be faithful. When facing God, results are not important. Faithfulness is what is important."

She says that she draws from this quote time and time again.

"Even when we fail, if we truly believe we are following God's call on our lives, then we need to persevere. Don't give up and write off your experience as a misstep from the will of God. You must continue on."

And, trust him they did, which allowed for a great many inspirational moments along the way.

Personal reflection - Susan

One winter evening, not long after John and I started the ministry, John mentioned that he needed to buy a new winter coat. When I asked what happened to the coat we had just bought, he told me that he gave it to one of our residents who didn't have a coat and had to walk about a mile in freezing temperatures to catch the bus.

After a moment of annoyance, I quickly realized something significant. God had honored us with the opportunity to give a coat to someone who legitimately needed one. How often are we close enough to a needy person to know exactly what that person needs and then be able to provide for that need?

To me it was an awesome lesson and an opportunity for love in action.

Inspiration in a truck

Sometimes inspiration comes in unexpected words of kindness or small acts of generosity. So it was for Vision House.

Anyone who runs a housing program knows that it demands a lot of manual labor, including repairs and ongoing maintenance. It also requires the transportation of a multitude of supplies and furniture.

Shortly after closing the women's program, it became clear that Vision House needed a truck because they were hauling so much furniture, bedding, and supplies from location to location. John and Susan considered asking their church for a donation, but upon further reflection, decided this request might be too big. They chose to pray for help instead.

"This journey involved one small miracle after another," says Susan. "And our prayers for a truck was one of them."

"Do not be anxious about anything, but in every situation, by prayer and petition, with thanksgiving, present your requests to God."
—Philippians 4:6

The very next day, a volunteer called asking if Vision House could use a truck. The truck ran well, and this gentleman was looking to give it as a donation! The truck lasted many years in service to the men and women served by Vision House.

John remembers a story of how God protected this miracle truck, along with a couple of curious kids. He was letting a resident use the truck to travel to and from work because her car had broken down. One day, she came running into the office all distraught. She said the truck had come out of gear and rolled into a ditch.

John ran out and saw the resident's two children sitting in the front seat scared to death. He then found out the real story: the woman had run into the house to get something and left the truck running. And sure enough, one of her children had pulled down the gear shift, and the truck had taken off backward down the parking lot.

At the time, the parking lot was filled with cars, and the truck could have easily run into one them, causing damage to the car and possibly injuring the two children inside.

But, once again, God was watching over them. As it turned out, the steering wheel was turned just enough to allow for the truck to miss the cars and roll down the parking lot drive and into the ditch. The only casualty was a light post.

When the need is too great to ignore

In those early days, John and Susan were holding down full-time jobs and Susan was recovering from the birth of their second child. They were operating out of the basement of their home, with Susan serving as the primary administrative support for the myriad of people calling in for housing and services.

While they operated their three transitional men's homes, they listened to heart-wrenching stories from so many people they *couldn't* serve.

"The stories were so hard to hear. Often, I felt so overwhelmed that I just wanted to hang up, or better yet, just not answer the phone!" says Susan. "I remember the desperation in their voices with some people calling every day, hoping we would have an opening."

Personal reflection–Susan

I still remember the first resident and her children in the new home and the positive changes they made in their lives. God was truly working in this woman's life. She had been living in a short-term shelter in the inner city with her daughter. During the interview with us, she seemed so desperate and uncertain of her future. But I heard later how excited she was when she was accepted into the Vision House program. Her relief and excitement made every late night and every sore muscle of mine well worth it.

Why was this so memorable?

Because this is the reason Vision House exists. They are in the business of giving people a second chance. We are told by Jesus to reach out and help the least of these. Most Vision House residents are coming out of very tough places spiritually, physically, and emotionally. The mission Vision House is to show how hearts can be healed through the love of Jesus Christ.

Unfortunately, they had to turn a lot of needy people away. Especially women. On many of those calls, the common themes were domestic violence, job loss, abandonment, or lack of an existing support system.

Yes, the need was great. And once again, they began to contemplate taking in women, but this time, women with custody of their children.

Doing their due diligence, they made calls to local service providers to assess the need before jumping in. They were overwhelmed by the response. Counselors were convinced the need was great and if a family program were to open, it would fill quickly.

> *"And we know that in all things God works for the good of those who love him, who have been called according to his purpose."*
> **—Romans 8:28**

Susan remembers, "Call after call led me to see the great need and to wonder if God might be leading us to bring our original vision to help mothers and children experiencing homelessness to life."

When word got out that Vision House was possibly considering opening a family program, counselors began to refer clients to them because resources were so scarce. Calls for help increased significantly, increasing John and Susan's motivation to open a home for single mothers and their children.

Before long, the couple once again partnered with HUD to obtain a house. After speaking to a group at their local church about this next step for Vision House, they were astonished by the outpouring of support. By the time they returned home that day, they had three phone calls from people pledging to help with the new program. Some committed financially, while others agreed to volunteer. It was the first time they had seen such an expression of care and concern for the homeless.

"God had touched their hearts," Susan says. "We felt encouraged and believed God's hand was upon the expansion."

In 1994, they launched their fourth home in a double-wide mobile home, this time to serve single mothers and their children experiencing homelessness. The mobile home was also acquired through HUD and located in the Cascade area of Renton. This allowed them to use the same model as with the previous homes—signing a five-year lease for $1 a year. At the end of five years, they would either need to purchase the home or return it to HUD.

Mobile home used to house the first women with children program.

The enthusiasm for this new program was so great that a few close friends from their church converged on the home one weekend to clean, mow the lawn, plant flowers, move in donated furniture, make the beds, and even scrub the toilets. Others agreed to help care for the children, lead Bible studies, and provide welcome packages of groceries, hygiene items, and household items.

Again, John and Susan felt humbled by God's incredible provision through His people. And, as the volunteers were leaving, the first family moved in carrying only a large suitcase and a few boxes of belongings.

While this all seemed like another miracle, John and Susan knew it was just God's good grace showing itself in the form of loving, giving people.

When you have competing priorities

Any working parent will tell you that finding quality childcare is a struggle. It becomes especially difficult when you are: a) a single parent, and b) don't have the resources to pay for it.

Soon after opening the single mother's home in Renton, Vision House staff realized that the lack of childcare was a major obstacle when working with families to become self-sufficient. These were people already down on their luck. They were working diligently to learn new skills, go to school, and/or go to job interviews to become employed.

But who would look after their children while they left to get the training and education needed to get out of poverty and become self-sufficient?

The competing priorities became a constant struggle, so Vision House began to brainstorm ways to meet the childcare needs of the families in their care.

They thought they had found a perfect solution by partnering with a local church. They would use the church facility during the week, while the church used it on the weekends. The plan was to make the childcare available to the community as well, to offset the operating costs.

But it was also important to Vision House that the childcare be more than a service provided by volunteers. Liability was an issue, and they wanted to be able to assure parents of the safety and quality of the service itself. That meant it had to be licensed.

Unfortunately, opening a licensed childcare facility in a church would require a major remodel that would cost thousands of dollars. Even if Vision House agreed to raise the funds for the remodel, they could not find a church willing to dedicate that much of their facility to an outside group.

So, the concept of adding childcare to their program was put on hold.

Where there's a will, there's a way

Susan's inspiring children's book

As the Vision House program grew, it was clear that something more permanent and efficient in the way of housing was required. After all, it was difficult to manage multiple buildings spread out over several cities.

But neither John nor Susan had ever learned about construction, let alone built a home of their own. Nor did they imagine they would ever be required to do so. After all, their goal was to manage a program for the homeless, never anticipating the need to learn a myriad of new skills, like reading an architectural plan or wielding a hammer.

But once you accept responsibility for something, necessity becomes your master.

Vision House had operated the single mothers' program for several years in the double-wide mobile home when it came time to either purchase the home or return it to HUD. Although it had served its purpose, it wasn't a desirable purchase to operate a program long term.

While away at a women's retreat that year, Susan began to believe that God was calling them to build a home from the ground up to serve these women. It seemed ridiculous under the circumstances, since they didn't own any vacant property and had no construction experience. And yet, it also seemed right.

When Susan returned home, she went to the library and found a few children's books on how to build houses. Yes, children's books.

She studied up and learned what a footing was and the difference between a joist and a truss. The couple began having conversations with the Vision House board about whether construction might be the direction the ministry needed to take.

As they studied the question of whether to build a facility for families, they contemplated the fact they now *owned* two of the HUD homes they operated for the men's program. Around the same time, they signed a couple of contracts to receive government funding to support their program.

But it wasn't long before they also realized these government contracts would jeopardize their ability to share the love of Christ with their clients and offer voluntary Bible studies and reading materials. The government says that when you accept a direct federal grant, you cannot use it to fund religious activities.

As an organization conceived on the idea of faith in Christ and the ability to use that faith to turn lives around, this was important to them.

So, the board began a lengthy debate about funding. Should they continue the path they were on, or sever ties with the government funding sources?

This was not an easy discussion. After all, they had already been successful using government money. And they had big plans to enlarge their space to help a greater number of people.

After substantial prayer and reflection, the board of directors voted unanimously to change their status and become a 501(c)(3) *religious* organization, which would allow for the ministry to fall under the federal and state laws that protect the rights of Christian agencies. Everyone felt this was an important move in order to stay true to their original calling of serving Jesus Christ through ministering to the less fortunate in the community. But it would eliminate government funding.

As they made this momentous decision, they had to immediately tackle a looming problem. They had already acquired government funding to purchase the Everett and Maple Valley men's homes. And now, because they could no longer accept government funding, they would need to terminate their existing government contracts and transfer ownership of these homes to non-Christian agencies.

Not only that, they were now faced with the challenge of raising private money. And as any good fundraising expert will tell you, that isn't easy if you've never done it before.

"We had a crisis of faith when we wondered how, and if, God could provide for us without the government funds," Susan recalls. "Could we continue to expand and operate the ministry? How were we going to move forward?"

At the same time, however, the board also voted to accept the proposed plan to construct a larger home to accommodate more women and children. And they decided to build the home without the use of any funds that would jeopardize their ability to hire Christian staff and share their faith with the clients.

The challenge was set.

They then launched four simultaneous campaigns to increase private funding:

1. A church community campaign to build relationships and educate local churches;

2. A business community campaign to develop relationships and support from local business owners;

3. A foundation campaign to identify potential funding sources; and

4. A "Hunt for Homes" campaign to replace the homes the agency would turn over to a non-Christian agency.

In the end, they were successful, and these campaigns showed them that God was faithful in meeting the ministry's needs. They received donations from churches, businesses, foundations, and individuals to meet ongoing operating and project expenses, proving they didn't need to rely on government funding.

They only needed to rely on God.

3

A NEW BEGINNING

In 1996, Vision House launched the new effort to build the single mothers' facility free from any restrictive funding by using an old-fashioned barn-raising model. They started with a few volunteers, some in-kind commitments, and a few hundred dollars from family and close friends.

First wall goes up

But when you accept the barn-raising model of construction, you are also accepting a plan that cannot rely too much on deadlines. Why? Because you are relying mostly on volunteers and donations, which are not predictable.

This was the case for this construction project. Over a two-year period, the Vision House staff worked hard to raise money, staging several fundraising events, sending out letters, writing grants, and soliciting donors. On April 5, 1998, Vision House held its official ground-breaking.

And, then, armed with the knowledge Susan had gained from reading those children's books on construction and building houses, she decided to take on the role of general contractor for the project. She didn't own the skills yet, but she had the willpower.

"I began to stumble my way through a complicated permitting and building process with some great volunteer advisors by my side," she says.

But she was also serving as the primary caregiver for their two young children, overseeing the administration of the Vision House program, and working as the case manager and volunteer coordinator for the small family program.

Now, she had taken on the monumental task of overseeing the building project, and John couldn't help. He was already doing double duty working full time for the DOC and as executive director of Vision House, overseeing the primary operations of the program.

As they headed into the building phase of the project, Susan also knew it would be a difficult summer with their young boys out of school and John working full-time. But she prayed that God would somehow work out a way that she could care for her sons while focusing on the building project.

And, lo and behold, she received what she believed to be a revelation!

There were four large trees, perfectly placed on the property meant for the family facility where they could build a tree house. Her father thought it was a great idea and provided the wood and lots of fun stuff to include in the tree house once it was done. The finished tree house would only stand about five feet off the ground, but the boys were thrilled with the prospect of having a tree house of their own. And, once it was finished, the tree house gave them a safe platform from which to watch the heavy equipment clearing the site and making it ready for construction. The perch also put them easily within Susan's view while she directed the heavy equipment operators.

"I knew they were safe and didn't have to worry. I felt so blessed that the boys didn't see our many trips to the site as drudgery but as a fun and exciting time."

A little prayer goes a long way

Sometimes we are called to do what seems impossible at the time. One such moment was during the construction of the new Renton women's and children's home, when Susan realized there was no way to get all the lumber up to the second floor without volunteers moving it by hand. This would be a difficult and time-consuming project.

But since prayer was a daily part of her routine, she reached out for help, and the project was blessed when someone offered to bring a forklift to the site to move the lumber. This was a prayer answered, and all seemed good.

That is, until on the appointed day, panic set in. Susan realized the second layer of subfloor hadn't been laid. She rushed to the site, knowing she had to find a way to get the subfloor down before the forklift arrived, otherwise the forklift would be useless and a wasted donation.

But how would she and her two small boys accomplish such a feat, when it was a job for four grown men?

"Start by doing what's necessary; then do what's possible; and suddenly you are doing the impossible."
—St. Francis of Assisi

"I really did begin to panic," she says. But she decided to pray for help instead. So she did. And she did it out loud for all the world to hear.

Immediately, a plan popped into her head. If she would just slide the large pieces of sheathing over to a platform, flip them up onto the platform with a two-by-four and then run up to the second floor and heave them up over the side of the building, she could do it.

And that's what she did, quoting as she went, "I can do all things through Christ who gives me strength!"

Watching her, the boys chimed in, singing their version of *High Hopes,* popularized by Frank Sinatra.

In this version, however, the kids replaced the word "ant" with "Mommy" and the "rubber tree plant" with "Jesus Christ."

"We laughed as I struggled," Susan remembers with a smile. "And the boys witnessed God's immediate answer to prayer firsthand."

Volunteers provided the fuel to run the engine

Because the Vision House board had decided on a barn-raising style of construction, there was a constant call out for volunteers. Slowly but surely, volunteers from local churches and community groups began to show up to lend a hand on nights and weekends. If they didn't have a skill, they learned it.

Susan tells the story of a young, single mother who arrived one day to volunteer, sharing the fact that she had just moved into a new Habitat for Humanity home herself. Because she felt so blessed by that miracle, she wanted to help others.

When Susan asked her if she brought any tools with her, the woman pulled out a small hammer normally used for picture-hanging. Susan just smiled and handed her an apron full of nails that were about the same size as the hammer she held in her hand, and the woman went to work.

Tiny hammer, big heart

"The sight of this incredible young woman hammering away next to people with framing hammers and nail guns has always stuck with me," says Susan. "It reminded me of the story in Mark, when Jesus called over his disciples to point out the poor widow who had just given a few coins. Giving out of her poverty was more meaningful to Christ than all the others who gave out of their wealth."

It wasn't long before a skilled volunteer noticed this woman struggling with her tiny hammer and gave her a little training with a nail gun. She quickly caught up with the rest of the skilled laborers.

Sometimes you just have to make the case

The new housing project had been under way for a little over a year when a major obstacle popped up, not unheard of in any major construction.

One of the final major tasks before they could move families in would be connecting the sewers. Unfortunately, there was a huge waterline in the middle of the road. They would have to avoid it when drilling under the road to connect the sewer to the other side of the street. The civil engineer on the project let Susan know that if they hit the waterline, it would most likely make national news.

It was that big of a deal.

The problem was they were having difficulty finding a contractor with the expertise needed to do the job. When they finally found the right contractor, John was on-site one night while the contractor was working on the sewers. They were using huge equipment to tunnel under the street to make the connection to the sewer line.

At one point, John heard some shouting and went outside to investigate. He saw the owner of the company arguing with his employees about the job not lining up correctly.

"He was essentially telling his crew that he was going to pack up and cancel the job," John says.

John knew that if these guys walked away, it would take several months to find another company capable of completing the work, which would significantly delay the opening of the shelter. John called Susan to fill her in on the situation, and she jumped in the car and headed to the construction site.

On her way there, she noticed a large yellow and red maple leaf gently floating down to hit the windshield. And it struck her that it was getting cold! Winter was around the corner, and they needed to get this shelter open so fewer kids would be sleeping in cars that winter.

A rage grew inside her. "This contractor isn't getting it," she thought. "He needs to get this sewer line in!"

She arrived at the site just in time to hear the boss yell at his crew that they were leaving. He approached her as he removed his gloves to let her know he was finished.

But in her head, she was thinking, "Oh, no you don't!"

When he came within her reach, she grabbed his arm, looked him in the eye and asked, "Do you see the leaves starting to change color? That means it is getting cold out, and mothers and young children are sleeping in their cars tonight. They'll be sleeping in the cold! We need to get this place open!"

She told him that he needed to figure out what the problem was and get the job done. He mumbled something back at her as he walked away, put his gloves back on, and yelled for his crew to get back to work.

And with that, the sewer was connected. The first residents moved in on December 23, 1999.

The 5,000-square-foot facility still stands today, built in less than 18 months, debt free, providing warmth and comfort to approximately 16 women and children each year.

Time for a change

During the time the first construction project was nearing completion, John realized that working full-time at the Snohomish County Corrections, commuting from Renton, and spending 15 to 20 hours a week with Vision House was all becoming too much of a struggle. Although his long-term goal was to work full-time at Vision House, he knew that resigning from a stable government position that included family benefits would require a huge step of faith. So, he began to work out how he could cut back his hours at the DOC, but still retain those important benefits.

Soon, Vision House received a small grant giving the organization a little breathing room to operate the ministry without the stress of worrying so much about money. But it wasn't enough to pay John. Then, a second grant came their way. This one was enough to allow them to operate the ministry through the end of the year, but it still wasn't enough to pay John a salary.

John continued to work his full-time job with the government while volunteering at Vision House. As he struggled to figure out how he could make a change in his job status work, he did the math and figured it would take about $15,000 above and beyond Vision House's general operating expenses for him to go part-time at the DOC.

And once again, God answered the call.

On June 15, 1998, Vision House was awarded a grant for $15,000— exactly. The grant allowed John to pursue a part-time position with the DOC. However, he was told that it would take several months to fill his current position.

Shortly after that, John's manager called to tell him that during his quiet time that morning, he felt the Lord telling him to let John formally reduce his hours. John's manager said, "As a Christian, I appreciate your desire to work with the homeless, and I want to do what I can to support you."

John started working part-time the next week, finally bringing some balance to the Camerer household. The following year, however, he was unexpectedly called back to work full-time again. The thought of him trying to work full-time and keep Vision House up and running was overwhelming to both him and Susan.

"This was another brief crisis of faith," says John. "The thought of supporting our family with an income based on grants, donations, and a small amount of rent collected from people in recovery scared us to death."

For the past 15 years, the Camerers had enjoyed the security of a government paycheck each month. They depended on that to give them the freedom to focus on the ministry. But if they weren't secure financially, how would they be able to continue their work with Vision House?

> *"Whoever watches the wind will not plant;*
> *whoever looks at the clouds will not reap."*
> **— Ecclesiastes 11:4**

"I had already resigned myself to the fact that our lives were going to be a little different than most," says Susan. "Conversations in our household and around our dinner table were about illegal drug use, prostitution, addiction, recovery, prison and jail terms, criminal behavior, violence, suicide and death, homelessness, and poverty."

As they contemplated this potential change in their lives, they realized their life was good. They weren't living on the street. They had a home, a decent salary, a couple of cars in the garage, and their children attended a private Christian school. That school was important to them given the type of clients they worked with and the ministry they were called to. They wanted to make sure their children had a solid understanding of why they had reached out to people who were hurting and how important it was to their faith to continue this work.

One day, while John was grappling with whether to quit the DOC, Susan sat in a large green reclining chair in the corner of their living room. They called it their "prayer chair." She prayed, letting God know that she really didn't want John to quit his job and go into the ministry full time.

"I was scared to death," she says. "Could God really care for the needs of our family if we chose to follow Him down such an uncertain path?"

But as she sat quietly thinking about their future, she was reminded that Christ tells us to "Love the Lord your God with all your heart and with all your soul and with all your mind." (Matthew 22:37). It was at that moment, she realized she was ready.

"Whatever He called me to do, I could do. I was willing to sell our cars, our home, live in a small apartment and yes, even take our kids out of the private Christian school to follow Him. He had made a change in my life, and I was prepared to be fully devoted to Him."

At the same time, John began to pray and seek God's will for his life. It became clear to him that God was calling him to take a huge step of faith; he would resign his position with the corrections department and join God fully in the place where He was already at work. John felt that God had been faithful over the past ten years in supporting men, women, and children experiencing homelessness in changing the direction of their lives through the Vision House program.

Now, he and Susan were being asked to rely completely on God to take care of their young family. This would be the first step in a new relationship they both had with God.

John and Susan had come to the same conclusion independent of each other. They would risk it all and follow the will of God.

They took their decision to the board of directors to inform them that John was feeling called to quit his job and work in full-time ministry. The board, however, had deep concerns about the extra financial burden John's salary would be on the ministry, while still covering other operating costs.

John and Susan presented their case and then were asked to step out of the meeting for 30 minutes so the board could address the issue. The half-hour turned into an hour and a half before they were called back in, a sure sign that this was a difficult decision.

The board did vote to allow John to go full-time starting the next month. It hadn't been an easy decision. One board member resigned as result, but John and Susan went home that night relieved and anxious for their future.

> *"...being confident of this, that he who began a good work in you*
> *will carry it on to completion until the day of Christ Jesus."*
> **—Philippians 1:6**

In the end, John and Susan didn't need to worry.

John went to their post office box the next day, Monday, to get the mail. He picked up a few donations, and then he found something very special. They received an unexpected check for $40,000!

John knew this check had to be in the mail prior to the board decision for it to have arrived on Monday. And, it was almost exactly the amount they needed to cover John's salary and operating expenses for a year.

Was this a coincidence? No. This was confirmation from God that they had made the right decision for John to start full-time at the ministry. God would provide if they were just obedient to His calling.

Soon after that, Susan was being interviewed by a local newspaper reporter. The reporter asked, "Who are you guys? Are you some of those Microsoft millionaires that retired and are now working with the homeless?"

Millionaires?

Susan remembers the moment well. "I just laughed and thought, nothing could be further from the truth!"

A program to serve all who needed help

Around this time, Vision House was looking to hire a case manager for the men's program. They interviewed a few candidates, but most were not qualified and had limited experience working with people in recovery.

Soon they received an application from a candidate with excellent qualifications. In fact, he was way over-qualified for the job, and they couldn't believe he was applying to work for their little startup ministry. He had a master's degree and had served as the national director for a large well-known international Christian ministry.

During the interview, John and Susan learned that this man had lost his position with the large organization he'd worked for due to some "secret" sins that had a hold over his life. Because of it, he was humiliated and disgraced and asked to resign from his prominent position.

As John and Susan discussed whether to hire someone with such notoriety, they came to the realization that Vision House was all about second chances, forgiveness, and the grace of God. If Vision House was the right place for the homeless, the poor, and people in recovery, why wouldn't it also be the place for a staff person who needed a second chance?

They decided to hire him, even though he came to work as a broken and humble man. His starting salary was a fraction of what he had earned in his previous position, but he came ready to serve during a critical time when Vision House needed a new direction and a solid ministry plan. He also brought strategic thinking, initiative, and experience that John and Susan just didn't have. So, while still working from the basement of their home, they all began to develop a strategy to take the ministry to the next level.

While Vision House had lost potential funding opportunities because they had made the change from being a charitable organization to a religious organization, they continued to be blessed with "human" capital that would serve them well.

Sometimes it's not about moving mountains, it's about moving homes

A part of the new Vision House strategy became the Hunt for Homes Campaign, with the goal to replace the homes they would lose due to the organization's change in status. A program through the Port of Seattle was giving away houses that needed to be moved to build a third runway for the airport. The price was right, so Vision House took one of the homes and began to look for a piece of property to place it.

The county had some surplus property near Sea-Tac airport and was willing to sell it at a greatly reduced rate to a non-profit looking to house homeless people. Bingo! Vision House put in a bid for $15,000 for the property, and their bid was accepted. Once again, they were off to their next building project.

They assembled a team of volunteers from a local church to help with the project. A teacher by the name of Jody Collins agreed to serve as the project coordinator. They called the home the Mustard Seed House after the verse in Matthew:

> *He replied, "Because you have so little faith. Truly I tell you,*
> *if you have faith as small as a mustard seed, you can say to this*
> *mountain, 'Move from here to there,' and it will move.*
> *Nothing will be impossible for you."*
> **—Matthew 17:20**

The Mustard Seed House

But now they had a new challenge. Had any member of the Vision House team ever moved an entire home? No. But move it they would.

"Seeing the house being hauled by a semitruck down the middle of the road on a couple of huge flatbeds, having to move power lines, mailboxes and signs in its way, I had a whole new understanding of what Christ meant when He said that our faith could move a mountain," says Susan.

And Susan remembers that asking Jody Collins to participate in this project was a miracle in and of itself.

Jody attended a small church that was full of the type of volunteers they needed to pull off a project like this, namely an architect, building designer, heavy equipment operator, building supply owner, general contractor, builder, and many more skilled laborers. The resources that God provided through Jody's little church were amazing.

One more small miracle

There was a point when the workers were pouring the foundation slab for this new home when God was called upon once more. All volunteers were "on deck" lending a hand to pour and shovel concrete. Men, women, children—it didn't matter who they were. There was a lot of work to be done, and they needed a lot of hands to do it.

The slab started under the house and then worked its way through the cutout for the door and finally ended outside. While everyone worked on the concrete inside, it began to pour one of those torrential downpours that sometimes happen in Seattle.

"Oh, man, we prayed," says Susan. "The kids prayed; everyone prayed that it would stop raining by the time we got to the outside slab. If not, the concrete would be ruined."

Again, by the grace of God, the rain stopped by the time they reached the door. And they finished the slab in the sun.

"Some may believe that it was just a coincidence, but I am not convinced that God doesn't control the weather just to increase the faith of a few," says Susan.

Lessons to be learned

We all know that much of life involves learning lessons the hard way. We face the challenge. We do not succumb. We gather our resources. And we overcome whatever the hardship may be. The goal, however, is to mark how we got there in the first place so that next time we avoid the challenge altogether.

The Mustard Seed House presented such a challenge to Vision House.

The Sea-Tac community was already in a fight against the building of a third runway at the airport, believing it would decrease their home property values. At the same time, several social service providers were eyeing property in the area because of the tremendous community needs and the availability of inexpensive property.

Unfortunately, community members had been placated by the promise of a small park on a vacant piece of property which people believed was owned by the parks department. The problem was that the property was *not* owned by the parks department. It was owned by the Washington State Department of Transportation . . .

. . . who then sold it to Vision House.

Yes, this put Vision House right in the line of fire.

So, when Vision House paraded the Mustard Seed House down the street right past the local elementary school and plopped it onto the property that people thought had been earmarked for a park expansion, the community erupted in outrage.

According to Susan, the Mustard Seed project seemed like the straw that broke the camel's back. Council members were fighting. County departments were angry. Community members feared the type of people housed by Vision House, thinking they would need to start carrying weapons to stay safe. Some folks even screamed obscenities at Vision House volunteers. Women were crying that their children were no longer safe. And television and newspaper reporters began to cover the story.

"I wondered, what we had gotten ourselves into?" Susan remembers. "It still makes my head spin just thinking about the circumstances around those events."

How do you heal a wound this big? John and Susan decided to gather community members together to talk about it.

"We began to assemble a community meeting to alleviate any fears people had toward the population we would be serving onsite," says Susan.

They brought together a panel of similar service providers, a council member, and a former Vision House client. John offered to serve as the Vision House spokesperson.

"We thought we would be addressing a small group of concerned citizens," says John.

But as they approached the elementary school where the meeting was to take place, they noticed a large number of cars turning into the parking lot. In the end, there were several hundred people packed into the auditorium, along with local television cameras and news reporters.

Fortunately, the crowd responded positively to Micah Wells, who had graduated from Vision House. Micah shared with the audience that they had no need to be afraid of the men who would be living in the home. These men were clean and sober and just trying to get their lives back together. Micah went on to share his testimony and how God had used Vision House to help his own life. He went on tell them how long he was clean and sober and what he was doing today. People were mesmerized by his story.

"You could hear a pin drop in the room while he was talking," says Susan.

In addition, one of the other service providers, who was from a much larger and more sophisticated local ministry than Vision House, handled audience questions with grace and a sense of calm. They even spoke to newspaper reporters and television cameras, never once assigning blame to Vision House.

"I always felt as if God put this group there because He knew they could handle the situation much better than we could," Susan says. "They supported us, spoke highly of Vision House, and even sent volunteers to the site later to help with construction. This was a true image of what a Christian social service agency should look like in the community."

The project moved forward without incident, and The Mustard Seed House still serves Vision House today.

But Vision House management learned an important lesson through this process: how important good public communication is *before* heading into a project. As a result, community notification and neighborhood meetings are now a regular part of any Vision House building project.

4

COLLABORATION AND PARTNERSHIPS ARE KING

By the turn of the new century, Vision House was successfully meeting its mission to bring women and children off the street and into safe and secure housing, while providing services to help them to start over. They were a respected resource in the fight to end homelessness and had gained a reputation for providing a solid program of recovery and transition.

And yet, it wasn't enough.

"There were still too many people falling through the cracks in the system," says Susan. "We couldn't just stop and say we'd done enough."

And so, in January of 2000, the Vision House board voted to launch a campaign to raise $1 million to build a second phase of the single mothers' complex in Renton.

John and Susan don't believe in coincidences. One day, a family friend, Lynda Hester, who worked for the Master Builders Association of King and Snohomish Counties, stopped by the Camerer's home to drop off Susan's son after a sleepover. Lynda told Susan that she wanted to learn more about the project they were working on.

Susan invited her in and soon discovered that she was serving as the interim director for the association's new startup foundation, HomeAid Master Builders Care. Lynda explained that they were searching for projects that supported families experiencing homelessness that also needed some expert volunteer building support.

Susan was skeptical and asked who would get the building once it had been built. Lynda told her that Vision House would.

"But who operates the program?" Susan asked.

"You do!" Lynda replied.

Both women realized this partnership could be the start of something big. Within days, Lynda had arranged to have national leaders fly in to meet with John and Susan to discuss how the partnership would work. In the end, Vision House and HomeAid partnered on several projects resulting in millions of dollars' worth of shelter beds being brought to the community.

Vision House has been blessed over the years with tremendous financial and volunteer support from local foundations and organizations. This includes the Master Builders Association of King and Snohomish Counties, along with a variety of local builders and vendors.

And, in 2001, in partnership with the Bill & Melinda Gates Foundation and the Master Builders Association of King and Snohomish Counties, Vision House finished construction of Phase II for mothers and their children, tripling capacity by adding an additional eight apartments.

Jay Wallace, another one of their many volunteers, remembers when they were about to prepare the land for Phase II of the Renton project. He says that when it came time to begin, the adjacent neighbors had hired someone to remove some of their trees. Susan had marked trees to be *saved* on the Phase II land. The contractor saw her markings, thought they were to be *removed*, and not knowing he was on the wrong property, cut them all down and left the neighbor's trees standing!

"Susan sobbed about those trees," says Jay. "In fact, it made the news."

However, this too was a blessing. The removal of the wrong trees opened the site up and made for a better site plan.

"It was an ugly, ugly time that turned into a beautiful thing," says Jay.

From moving mountains to scaling them

It was time for Vision House to tackle the childcare problem.

In 2003, Vision House initiated the Campaign for Children's Village which would raise $6.6 million to add 11 transitional housing units that included a licensed childcare center for 88 children, counseling offices, and administrative space within walking distance of its first single mothers' complex in Renton, Washington.

The capital campaign began in 2004, led by the city of Renton's then-mayor, Kathy Keolker, concurrent with the design phase of the Children's Village complex. This was a major project. But with the support of Conner Homes, Sajasa Construction, and HomeAid Master Builders Care, Vision House opened four housing units and a childcare center for 88 children in June of 2005.

Then, in 2005, Vision House participated in a reality television show called *Home Team*. Within the tradition of old fashion barn-raising, each week friends, families and communities would join in presenting a deserving family with their first home.

The Vision House project was to be a bit outside of the show's normal format by building a project to support local transitional housing. Vision House was bursting at the seams and was in desperate need for additional program space and counseling offices for the children's program.

The staff enjoyed a few minutes of fame as they worked alongside Schneider Family Homes to complete a resident community center (Schneider Family Playroom) that included teen hangout space, a computer center, counseling space, and appropriate activity space for children of all ages.

Then, in the Spring of 2007, with the support of CamWest Development and HomeAid Master Builders Care, Vision House began construction on the HEDCO Building in Renton, which would provide housing for an additional four families. Later that Fall, with the support of Centex Homes and HomeAid, Vision House began construction on the agency offices, program space and three additional housing units for families experiencing homelessness.

Vision House battled through the great recession in partnership with the HomeAid Master Builders Care and CamWest Development and completed construction on the HEDCO building in May of 2008. Four new families moved in, bringing the number of apartment units Vision House operated at that time to 20.

Eight storage garages were also part of the HEDCO building, allowing Vision House to store donations of furniture, clothing, and household items. Vision House also continued operating a separate program serving nine men in recovery from drug and alcohol addiction.

By the end of 2008, Vision House had served nearly 600 men, women and children experiencing homelessness in its 19 years of existence. And, almost 90 percent of Vision House residents had transitioned to permanent housing and a better way of life.

In 2009, Centex Homes completed the third and final building in the Children's Village complex, which added three more family housing units, an afterschool program, counseling, and administrative offices.

"When I look back on those 19 years," says Susan, "I feel tired but filled with immense joy."

John adds, "We did what we started out to do. It wasn't easy, but then God doesn't call you because things are easy."

Reflection—John Camerer

Vision House dedicated itself early on to building debt-free. This allowed for dollars to be spent on operating programs instead of servicing debt. As a result, often the buildings and capital campaigns took a little longer than anticipated.

A construction company may generously volunteer their crews when paid work is lacking to keep the crews busy. But when a paying job comes up, they need to take it. After all, there are bills to pay and mouths to feed. This means the company needs to put their philanthropic work on the back burner for a while. Although this makes managing a construction timeline more difficult and requires more patience, Vision House's philosophy has been that they would rather wait for volunteer availability instead of running out and paying someone who could get the job done more quickly.

This serves two purposes. First, Vision House stretches their construction budgets. Secondly, the company donating their service feels good about the donation because they are not pressured to finish by a hard deadline. The debt-free philosophy has also given Vision House a sense of peace, since they aren't racing against high-interest loan payments.

5

JACOB'S WELL

"Let us not become weary in doing good, for at the proper time we will reap a harvest if we do not give up."
—Galatians 6:9

In 2002, Kurt and Craig Campbell became part of the Vision House story.

Craig and Kurt own the Campbell Auto Group in Edmonds, Washington. Kurt said, "I had recently confirmed my life to the Lord and had struggled to bring the body of Christ together."

So, he and his brother invited eight local pastors to meet at their dealership. The purpose of the meeting was to build relationships, pray, and begin to identify community needs. The guest list represented all different denominations, and only one individual on the list was known to them.

Four of the invitees showed up to the meeting. As they went around the room to express what each of them thought was the greatest need in their community, to a person, they answered that there was a real need for transitional housing for moms and their children experiencing homelessness.

Once a consensus was reached within the group, no one knew how to proceed or what to do to bring their dreams to fruition. Fortunately, the Campbell brothers had recently visited Vision House in Renton and suggested a field trip.

The group traveled to Renton to experience first-hand what Vision House had to offer families experiencing homelessness. The trip was a success *and* an inspiration. The visiting group felt that Vision House was an appropriate model of Christian transitional housing, providing supportive services these families. They asked if Vision House would be interested in partnering with them to replicate their program in Shoreline.

The answer was yes. All this was God's way of bringing like-minded people together to do good things and yet remain anonymous.

Expanding faith

Once they'd made the decision to move forward with the Jacob's Well project, Kurt Campbell remembers thinking, "Wow, the difficult part is that this will take a lot of money and a lot of hands on deck."

Undeterred, in 2009, Susan asked Kurt to chair a fundraising campaign, something he'd never done. The goal was to construct a transitional housing complex that would include 20 apartments and a childcare center, along with counseling and program space for families experiencing homelessness.

And with that, the journey to build Vision House Jacob's Well began.

According to Susan, 2009 was a difficult time to obtain funding. It was at the height of the recession, and nearly every major funding organization had declined their requests. It wasn't because of the merit of the proposal. As Susan says, "The plans were solid, and the need was great."

But even the funding sources didn't have the wherewithal to grant the requests. All over the region the need was great. Competition for funds was fierce, and funds were limited.

"Even funding sources with which we had signed letters of agreement to the tune of several hundred thousand dollars had let us know they wouldn't be able to fulfill their pledge commitments," says Susan.

Their funding plan collapsed.

People did become discouraged, even a little weary. But their enthusiasm and faith in the Shoreline project never faltered. In fact, the board felt their direction was clear and that they had been called to move forward on a primarily volunteer basis.

Susan remembers referring to a passage in Isaiah repeatedly during that time to keep her motivated.

Do you not know? Have you not heard? The LORD is the everlasting God, the Creator of the ends of the earth. He will not grow tired or weary, and his understanding no one can fathom. He gives strength to the weary and increases the power of the weak. Even youths grow tired and weary, and young men stumble and fall; but those who hope in the LORD will renew their strength. They will soar on wings like eagles; they will run and not grow weary, they will walk and not be faint.
–Isaiah 40:28-31

Susan would remind herself often that God did not get tired of His effort to build shelter for moms and kids experiencing homelessness in Shoreline. In fact, had HE not stated that HE was the father to the fatherless and defender of widows? And wouldn't a father love His children and have a strong desire to protect and provide for them?

"I knew that He did," says Susan. "And I believed that during that time period more than ever."

The early days of the Jacob's Well project were difficult. That period reminded Susan about the first shelter they had built in Renton. They had begun with almost nothing: a few key volunteers and about $400 donated primarily from Susan's mom and sisters. Regardless, they felt compelled to plunge ahead, and not long after the sun began to shine on them. Church and community volunteers began to show up. Momentum built. And things began to roll.

But as had often been the case in the first Renton project, the Shoreline project soon ran into a snag. They had just over $1,000 in the bank and had hired a small company to do the damp-proofing on the foundation wall.

"I knew the bill would be right around $1,000," Susan remembers.

Up to this point, everyone Susan had hired to complete a paying job was asked for a deep discount on the price and/or to donate their services. This became an exhausting exercise for her as well as for the contractors. But it was important to stretch every cent.

As she was on her way to pay the gentleman for his damp-proofing, Susan began to struggle with whether she should ask him for a discount. After all, it was getting tiresome to begin every conversation with, "Is there any chance you can do this for free or at least a reduced rate?"

So, once again, Susan turned to God for help and guidance. She wanted God to know that this man also had a family to support. He was a small business owner and was just trying to make ends meet like everyone else.

After a bit of a struggle, she concluded, "God, I am just NOT going to ask him for a discount. I am going to pay that bill, the full price. That settles it!"

As this kind gentleman was packing up his equipment, he asked for more information on the project. Typically, Susan had her two young sons with her, so contractors assumed she was building a family home.

"But considering this one had two kitchens, 10 bedrooms, two offices and five bathrooms, they must have wondered how many MORE kids I had," she remembers, laughing.

She told this man that she was building a shelter where moms and kids experiencing homelessness could rebuild their lives. He went to his truck to prepare the invoice, and when he returned, he handed her an invoice that read, "No charge."

She was shocked. But the man said, "My wife was a single mom before I married her. I want you to know I support what you are doing. I know it is really tough being a single mom."

"I was so humbled," Susan says.

I realized that God had a plan. He was going to build the shelter no matter what. I just needed to follow Him, seek His guidance, and have faith."

She decided right then and there that that was how they would get the Jacob's Well project in Shoreline built. They would raise a little money, build a little, raise a little more, and build a little more. It would be done in phases, with God at their backs.

It wouldn't be easy. Planning would be difficult. But they had done it twice before with success, and those buildings are still standing today.

Workers pray as they do God's work for Jacob's Well.

A series of prayer events was orchestrated, and their old-fashioned barn-raising strategy was deployed once again, leveraging volunteer help.

In 2010, thanks to a $266,000 grant for site improvements from the HEDCO Foundation, Vision House was able to break ground on Jacob's Well in Shoreline, Washington, and work on the new facility began.

"Our faith grew as we saw God's obvious hand of provision every day," Susan says.

The next year, Vision House put out messages to local churches that they needed help in building the facility.

"The dealership propelled everything," says Craig Campbell. "It was through the dealership that we spread the word to all churches and to people inside the church."

Ted and Becky Almquist were two of the people who attended a meeting facilitated by the group. At the meeting, attendees were given an opportunity to sign up to assist in the building of Jacob's Well. Contractors had already been assigned, and volunteers could sign up for different aspects of the construction project.

The meeting was well attended. It consisted of 30 volunteer professional leads including builders, engineers, architects, project managers, general contractors, 100 or so skilled carpenters, and countless general laborers all excited to help.

"I signed up to help with construction," says Ted, "while Becky volunteered to help with administrative work."

Susan says it was a massive, coordinated effort. An incredible volunteer, Craig Hawkins, stepped up to take the lead, and more than 600 volunteers framed the three-story, 20,000-square-foot structure over the course of a few weekends.

"Now it was our turn," says Ted Almquist. "The professionals would go back to their own jobs and volunteers would continue and work with the volunteer general contractor, Bob Sime."

Bob Sime had just retired as a general contractor and learned through his church about the project.

"There were four general contractors," he says. "And three had businesses to run."

They began with the framing and foundation, and when the business contractors had to go back to their companies, Bob did the finish work with a team of volunteers. He says that 90 percent of them didn't know what they were doing, so he would spend time at the beginning of each day explaining the individual tasks.

Volunteers frame Jacob's Well.

"In fact, two of the guys that were there almost every day," says Bob, "were Ted Almquist and Don Ricker. Ted was an eye doctor and Don was a banker, but they were willing to try anything."

A lot of people showed up with their own equipment, and some of the contractors would loan equipment to the project. Much of the professional work was donated, like drywall and window installation. But they did hire and pay electricians and plumbing contractors, and Bob helped to oversee it all.

"Bob worked tirelessly, Wednesday through Saturday, for almost three years, coordinating volunteers, vendors, and subs to bring the project through to fruition," says Ted.

In 2012, while their work was overseen by Mr. Sime, the smaller group of dedicated volunteers accomplished a long list of construction jobs beyond framing, including insulation, drywall, taping, spackling, finish carpentry, siding, and fencing. They even constructed the children's play yard.

Even if you didn't know how to handle a hammer, there was a job for you.

> ***A generous person will prosper;***
> ***whoever refreshes others will be refreshed.***
> **—Proverbs 11:25**

"Part of my job," says Becky, "was to check in construction volunteers and make sure they had all the proper paperwork and safety gear."

Bob's wife, Roberta, helped to provide lunches. Sometimes she made the food, sometimes she brought sub sandwiches or pizza to the guys working on the site.

"They were always happy to see me," she said.

Roberta also helped with the fundraising. Once the first phase of the project was completed, her church group furnished and decorated one of the rooms.

It would take three years to complete, largely due to the barn-raising model.

"There were times when the whole project was on hold waiting for funds or for the subcontractors," Bob says.

For instance, there was a long wait for the elevator because the company was donating the installation and they had to service their paying customers first.

"Also," says Bob, "the project began during the recession and construction companies were sitting around idle. Then, suddenly, things got busy and those companies had to resume working with paying customers and would come to Jacob's Well only when they could spare the time."

Then, of course, as with any construction project, there were problems that arose along the way that slowed it down.

Blessed is the one who perseveres under trial because, having stood the test, that person will receive the crown of life that the Lord has promised to those who love him.
—James 1:12

"We were close to completion and a big opening celebration had been scheduled," Becky Almquist reports. "But one day the sprinkler system broke and shot water everywhere."

Suddenly, they had to get pumps in to dry everything out and then replace drywall.

"We had to redo drywall two feet up from the floor on half the offices," Ted Almquist says.

This was a discouraging setback, forcing the opening to be delayed.

But, in 2014, the first of two Jacob's Well buildings was completed, providing 12 apartments for moms and children experiencing homelessness, counseling offices and children's program space. Next up, Vision House obtained their occupancy permit and then once again, put out a call for help.

To control costs, Vision House asked individuals, businesses, or nonprofits to "adopt a room" and provide furnishings to welcome families. The call was answered, and furniture, bedding, toiletries, kitchen utensils, and cookware were donated to help families get the best start possible.

Becky Almquist also answered the call. "I adopted a three-bedroom apartment on behalf of Alderwood Community Church," she says.

Her church also supplied windows and other necessary materials, and several of the men from church were part of the volunteer group.

"This was a labor of love for all of us," says Becky.

According to Ted Almquist, the goal was to make the women and children who would move in feel good about themselves.

He says, "If you take it from a mom's or kid's standpoint after living in a car, the apartment we gave them looks like a room at the Ritz Carlton. They can get a start on restoring their lives, and you hope you helped them in some small way make a positive change."

According to Kurt Campbell, from inspiration to completion, it would take ten years to complete Jacob's Well, with the help of more than 50 churches, 150 businesses, and 1,000 volunteers.

Phase II of Jacob's Well

In 2015, the board began to have serious discussions about an expansion at Jacob's Well. They called on donors and volunteers and gathered letters of support to determine whether the timing was right to launch the construction of the second phase.

The board approved plans to build an additional eight apartments and a childcare center in Shoreline, and the HEDCO Foundation once again committed over $96,000 to build this critical additional housing.

HomeAid Puget Sound identified builder captain, Polygon NW Homes, to build Jacob's Well, Building B. After a long delay in the permitting process, Vision House finally broke ground in April of 2018 and began construction in August.

Plans were reworked to add an additional two apartments for a total of 10, with six two-bedroom apartments and four three-bedroom apartments to provide housing for larger families—a huge need in transitional housing. A much-needed additional childcare facility was also included.

It was always about them

Unlike other transitional housing programs that merely move families in and then move them out, Vision House committed early on to send residents off to their new, permanent housing with everything they needed to continue their forward path. That meant they might take furniture, bedding, towels, and kitchenware with them.

"It's always been about the residents and how to give them a solid beginning," says Becky Almquist.

This is where volunteers like Becky picked up the slack. She took charge of supply replenishment when people moved out. "We called it 'flipping' the apartment," she says.

There was a little room on the first floor of the building we used for storage, she told us. It had everything from artwork to rugs to shower curtains and kitchen utensils. When a current resident moved out, staff would determine what they could take, and then volunteers would inventory what was left and go to the storeroom to replace it.

They accepted donations but would also buy needed items. This was another way the community could help. Local churches, businesses and groups would often hold drives for things to fill the gaps in inventory.

But that's not all Vision House provided. They had a mini-grocery store and small clothing bank where residents could shop.

"We've become rather well-acquainted with the local thrift stores, too," says Becky. "We'd shop at those places to replenish the apartments."

However, because people continued to donate items, the Almquists say that storage space became an issue, and they have now filled a couple of bedrooms in their own home with donated items.

The difference we make

When asked what he tells others about Vision House Jacob's Well now, Craig Campbell emphasizes how it's a place for single moms, single dads, and their kids, who really need a safe place to live while they get back on their feet. But he also emphasizes that Vision House is there with a full supportive and holistic approach.

In other words, it's not just housing. Through case management, education, and classes, Vision House helps with everything from finance to parenting and childcare.

"All those things" says Kurt Campbell, "need to work together for families to be self-sustaining."

But even with all that work, Craig admits that what they offer at Jacob's Well, "sometimes feels like a drop in the ocean based on the need that's out there."

Ted Almquist is also aware of the problem. He says, "If you look at the homeless situation and generational homelessness and what you can do to intervene, the need is overwhelming. And Vision House is dealing with a teacup."

So, if homelessness is such an enormous problem and so pervasive that it seems impossible to solve, why do so many volunteers give so much time, effort, and personal treasure for this project?

Because, says Kurt Campbell, "Vision House empowers those who are powerless. They come alongside vulnerable parents and kids and help rehabilitate them to get jobs and get on their feet. And they give them enough time to do that. To me that's what is critical in the whole housing world. The homeless need to be able to take care of themselves and not fall back into homelessness. And that takes time."

In fact, when asked if there was a solution to end homelessness, the National Alliance to End Homelessness replied, "Yes. To end homelessness, the nation will need an adequate supply of housing that is affordable to lower income households."

But Vision House has proven that housing alone isn't enough. A program that offers wraparound or support services is more successful.

Besides providing safe and secure housing, they also provide emotional support, education, skill-building, childcare, and more.

Why is this important?

Vision House helps to break down the systemic barriers these families face every day in trying to get back on their feet. Barriers that, on their own, would halt many of these families in their tracks and triple the likelihood their efforts would fail.

How does Vision House accomplish this?

1. With Vision House, families have a voice in their path forward and a choice in how they participate, so that each case management plan is personalized.

2. Residents are supported by a team of staff and volunteers who have their best interests at heart.

3. Vision House collaborates with other nonprofits and social service agencies to support clients and bring additional resources to the table.

4. Individualized plans capitalize on each resident's strengths and are supplemented by teaching the life skills necessary to be successful long-term.

5. The program is inclusive, so that individual beliefs and traditions are honored.

6. The entire program is dependent on the morals and values inherent in the teachings of Christ.

Jay and Diana Wallace became involved because they knew John and Susan through a church care circle back in 1990. Since Jay was an architect, he volunteered to help make the early homes accessible for those with disabilities. As an occupational therapist, Diana served as one of the first case managers for women.

"There's always a bigger picture," she says. "Case-managing was hard. The choices the residents would make were tough. And sometimes you have to remind yourself that this isn't always pretty."

But Diana knew that this was for a long-term gain. So, like everyone else, she stuck with it.

So did Jay. He designed the first Renton buildings where families could share common areas. Later, Diana expanded her volunteering to integrate occupational therapy concepts such as songs and movement with the preschool kids.

"It feels wonderful to see the successes and to be doing the right thing for God," she says.

And isn't that the true nature of volunteerism? Showing how all lives have value?

Because we care so much

Opening day at Jacob's Well

When asked about his favorite Vision House story, Kurt Campbell was quick to say, "My favorite moment was the finish line. We had organized all the volunteers to come for a ribbon cutting, and I was asked to say a few words. It's a three-story facility, and everyone was lined up along all the railings on each floor. When I got up to speak, I looked up at these hundreds of people who had worked as one to make this happen, and I can't describe the feeling. It was the highlight of my life."

"Consider those lives turned around," says Ted Almquist. "The Vision House success rate is amazing."

Sometimes there's even a more personal success story, such as when one of the moms and one of the men from Jacob's Well took jobs at an auto dealership owned by Kurt and Craig Campbell.

"It was nice to see first-hand how they went from homelessness to transitional housing to getting a job," says Kurt.

How do the volunteers feel who helped to build Jacob's Well?

"I feel blessed," says Becky Almquist.

"I think that's a good word for it," agrees Ted. "You just feel rewarded. Thankful that we could be a part of it and play some role in the happiness of those kids."

"What we did was fulfilling," says Craig Campbell. "Obviously, giving back to the community and leaving it a better place and a better community brought tremendous joy and satisfaction to us."

And Kurt's sentiments are more global. He says, "It makes me feel part of a greater good and gives me hope in mankind. In the end, it increases my faith."

6

LEADERSHIP TRANSITION

John and Susan decided early on that they would be careful to stagger their transitions away from Vision House when the time came for each of them to leave. They felt that if both founders left at the same time, it might raise concern from their funding sources, as well as the community, that things at the agency were unstable.

In 2015, after 25 years in leadership at Vision House, Susan decided the time had come to step away and start her own real estate company. John, however, would stay on as director of operations.

At the time, the board discussed launching a national search for a new executive director, but Susan felt strongly that the appropriate candidate was already on staff.

Enter Melissa Gehrig.

Melissa had come to Vision House 11 years prior as a single mom, looking for a flexible job that would allow her to care for her two children. She started as an office manager, was promoted to human resources manager, and along the way acquired her master's degree in Organizational Leadership.

Melissa had already become an integral part of the Vision House management team. She understood the culture, was a natural servant leader, and loved the staff that she had shepherded for so many years as the human resources manager.

Susan believed she was a perfect fit. When Melissa was offered the interim position of executive director, however, she wasn't sure. But as she walked to the car, she felt God say to her, "This is what I've equipped you for."

While the board was considering bringing someone in from the outside, Melissa says that as HR manager, she knew in intimate detail how much attention had been paid to hiring the kind of people who fit into a culture they had meticulously crafted.

She says, "My heart was heavy about that, so I felt God calling me to step up."

And she did. According to Susan, she did so effortlessly.

While a few major funders expressed concern that Vision House fundraising efforts might take a hit with the leadership change, Melissa was bound and determined that would not happen. First, she developed a strong support team. Then, she got on the phone and began calling and introducing herself to donors. She attended national conferences and even flew to California to meet face to face with an important major funder.

"The ministry did not miss a beat under Melissa's leadership," says Susan. "And it has gone on to launch its largest capital campaigns, its most aggressive building expansion, and received record-setting financial contributions."

Hiring Melissa to replace Susan was a win-win for everyone and allowed Susan to move on to new ventures confident that her "baby" was in good hands.

Employing a unique program model

In 2016, Vision House incorporated something called "trauma informed care" as the key component in its support program. The concept means that staff would be trained to be aware of the level of trauma each new client had experienced before coming to Vision House. This was important so that *how* staff interacted with that client didn't retrigger his or her traumatic experience.

"The concept," says Melissa, "can be as simple as not closing and blocking a door when you're in your first meeting with a client, because that can feel threatening. The client needs to feel safe and have the ability to walk away."

The Vision House program is also considered a "strength-based" program. This means that clients are helped to identify their strengths and past successes in order to focus on the best way to develop goals and necessary skills training to move forward.

What prompted these changes?

"I tell people that I didn't know anything about homelessness when I took over," Melissa tells us. "So, I spent a year in homeless bootcamp."

She says she talked to everyone she could, went to conferences, worked with mentors, and spent time with the Vision House program director to evaluate whether they were working to end homelessness with a family or inadvertently maintaining it.

"Because after all," she says, "the goal should be for the client to leave and not come back," Melissa said.

For instance, they did some pilot testing on eviction prevention and rapid re-housing, which strives to get the homeless into housing first. But they found that neither approach gave clients the essential time they needed to heal. The clients focused more on the money they would receive and not as much on the offers of life-changing supportive services.

Instead, Vision House staff decided to tell clients they would help them focus on a housing plan while getting services, then identify their barriers and develop a plan to equip them to maintain permanent housing.

Relationships are key

"Vision House is all about building relationships," Melissa says. "In fact, the staff works on building relationships before the clients even arrive."

And after they leave, the staff continues to support them. The relationship continues.

"We work hard on our internal culture, making it one in which people care about each other," Melissa is quick to say. "The uniqueness of what we do comes from our faith and our culture. We are always building relationships."

Melissa learned that homelessness is in large part a relationship issue and not a resource issue. She discovered this after working with mentor Jeff Lilly, then-executive director of the Seattle Union Gospel Mission.

She says that she and Jeff collaborated a lot on the idea that clients do need housing and employment, but first and foremost, they need to build positive, supportive relationships, which most of them don't have. Their relationships are broken or even toxic. But when they can rebuild or establish good relationships, then they will have the kind of backup they need when things go wrong.

Vision House volunteers are impressed with its programs, which is what keeps them so committed to their cause.

"Part of what I love is that they allow up to two years for the transitional housing," Mike Young, a volunteer tells us. "This gives families enough time to heal. They also provide all-around help and support to moms, including education, financial help, parenting skills, and childcare."

Volunteer Jay Wallace says he appreciates that the Vision House program isn't just putting on a bandage. He says that it is building accountability by building skills.

"We also added a diversion program," Melissa reports. "This is the entry point to Vision House and aims to divert a family from entering the shelter system in the first place by having a conversation with us before they come here."

The goal with the diversion program is to help the client identify other potential sources for stability they could rely on, such as family and friends, so they aren't forced into the shelter system. If other resources are identified, then Vision House helps them take advantage of those resources, even paying for bus trips or financial support, if needed.

"If it's clear that they need to come here, then we get them on an active participation list, which means they are getting started on some of the things they need to do, like counseling or entering a recovery program, before they come to us," says Melissa.

Vision House also has an alumni program, which follows clients who have left the program and helps them to stay on track. This keeps the recidivism rate low.

When you talk with John, Susan, or Melissa, you are also quick to understand how important the volunteers and staff are to their program.

"We've been able to engage volunteers in new ways," says Melissa.

Volunteers now teach life skills classes, help with literacy and cooking, and even serve as mentors for clients.

"Our volunteers have always been invaluable," Susan says. "We couldn't have accomplished anything we've done without them."

Melissa adds, "Our staff is first-class. But so are our volunteers. Together, they are the glue that holds everything together."

It has always been a concern of the Vision House leadership to create an environment that gives back as much as it takes from their staff.

"When I was HR manager," Melissa says, "I always told people that I was not the one doing the hard work, I was the one caring for staff so they could do the hard work. That's the culture here. One of care and self-care."

7

SERVING OTHERS

"Each of you should use whatever gift you have received to serve others, as faithful stewards of God's grace in its various forms."
—1 Peter 4:10

America relies on volunteerism, or the act of giving back to the community without the expectation of personal reward or recognition. In fact, volunteering dates to 1736, when Benjamin Franklin developed the first volunteer fire station to protect the community.

Since then, volunteers have played a strong role in America's ability to keep our communities healthy and strong.

How do they do this?

Volunteers enrich our lives by giving of themselves to beautify our parks, serve as local museum docents, raise money for worthy causes, mentor struggling students, write newsletters, or keep the books for small nonprofits, and lend their time and labor to build housing for the homeless.

Over 77 million people volunteered in the United States during 2018, and the estimated economic benefit was $167 billion.

Bargain Bash raises money for Vision House programs.

It's clear that Vision House would not exist as it does today in helping the homeless if it weren't for the hundreds of volunteers who have dedicated their time and effort to this cause, and continue to do so. And many of these volunteers will say they don't do it begrudgingly, or out of obligation. No, they volunteer because they feel blessed in their own lives and feel a duty to their community and to their faith to give back.

Going above and beyond

Many volunteers choose to only donate their time to support a nonprofit's mission. Others go above and beyond by lending more than time; they lend their talent and expertise as well.

Sylvia Holden was just such a volunteer. According to Susan, Sylvia was responsible for two very important components of the Vision House growth. First, she worked to implement a high-level policy governance model for the board of directors that is still being used today. The Vision House Board has been highly successful over the years, not only making tough decisions, but leading the organization to new heights.

Second, Sylvia coordinated an annual fundraising event called Bargain Bash, which started at her home as a yard sale that raised a few thousand dollars each time for Vision House programs. Just as important as the money were the items the event brought in that could be used by the residents. Things like pots and pans, clothing, bedding, toys, and furniture that helped to stretch Vision House operating dollars.

The Bargain Bash grew over the years to the point that it was moved onto the Vision House campus in Renton. The effort mobilized scores of volunteers, working hundreds of hours each year to pull off what had now become a community-wide effort, raising thousands of dollars for the agency.

Although the event raised significant revenue, the fact that it was held right on the Vision House campus made it clear that things like client confidentiality and safety, especially for the children in the childcare center, were being jeopardized with the crowds of shoppers coming to campus.

Therefore, Vision House made the difficult decision to shut down the Bargain Bash, and volunteers began to look for other ways to make up for the lost revenue. Sylvia helped to lead the effort to convince Vision House they needed to open a thrift store. Raising startup money, however, was out of the question since the ministry was in the middle of a capital campaign to build more housing units.

But volunteers did not give up easily. Soon it was discovered that Bellevue Christian School was looking to offload their thrift store in Bothell because it no longer matched their mission. Volunteers got wind of it and were convinced that it would be a match made in heaven for Vision House.

Soon after, the board agreed to take over operation of the store, inheriting a highly qualified manager, her staff, all the inventory, and an expensive point-of-sale soft-ware system. Nordstrom sent out a high-level executive to assist with marketing, merchandising, design, and inventory. She rolled up her sleeves and jumped right in alongside the other volunteers. Vision House was now the proud owner of a thrift store and it was up and running successfully.

Vision House operated the thrift store in Bothell for four years, but when rent was raised to a level that threatened profitability, the store was relocated to Renton, closer to the main Vision House campus. The store was also expanded to include a large warehouse where furniture and housewares could be processed and placed in the units as needed.

The thrift store is still an integral part of Vision House and saves tens of thousands of dollars each year in in-kind contributions, while still bringing in revenue to support programs.

The thrift store raises funds for Vision House and provides supplies for residents.

The personal payoff

People volunteer for all sorts of reasons. Sometimes, it's because someone they know asked them. Sometimes, it's to fulfill an obligation. Or it could be to meet new people or deploy a retired skill.

And there are many reasons volunteering is good for people. For instance, it's been proven that volunteering is good for your health. It combats depression and gives purpose. It connects you to others and increases self-confidence. It's also good if you're building your career because you learn new skills and can develop a resume. You can even network with professionals and businesses.

But volunteering can also bring fun and fulfillment to your life; it makes you feel good.

For example, Craig Campbell, who was instrumental in bringing Jacob's Well to life in Shoreline, says, "Volunteering for this project was fulfilling. Obviously, it's important to give back to the community and to leave it a better place." But he goes on to say that volunteering with

Vision House, "brought me joy and satisfaction to see such great things take place."

Sylvia Holden is one of those types of volunteers. She says, "Volunteering with Vision House has become a part of my life and has expanded and contracted over the years."

And, Ted Almquist says that working with Vision House has been, "life-changing."

But throughout the Vision House projects, both in Renton and in Shoreline, faith and a deep belief in God was a strong component in bringing such devoted people to the cause.

Jay Wallace says, "I tell people that if you have a heart for the homeless, Vision House is a fabulous place to change people's lives."

Roberta Sime says that when her husband retired, they prayed about what he would do next. And suddenly, the Vision House project popped up.

"We felt blessed when we heard about the opportunity," she remembers.

"I was Associate Pastor at Lake Forest Park Presbyterian Church," says Mike Young. "Several people from our congregation got deeply involved with Vision House, and so did I. We had a small congregation and yet ended up donating over 2,000 hours."

During the Jacob's Well project, Bob Sime says, "There was no competition between volunteers. People were there to do God's work and weren't looking for any sort of recognition or remuneration."

In fact, Bob said that it was a whole new experience for him because people working on Jacob's Well *wanted* to be there. When he was a paid contractor, it seemed that nobody wanted to work. They were always looking to go home early. But the volunteers at Jacob's Well had a good attitude, even though they weren't getting paid.

Bob's wife says that he would come home and say, "Everybody was happy and working today."

Tim Berg, another volunteer, says, "I enjoyed it because not only are you doing something good for the community, but there's a sense of camaraderie, and it's actually kind of fun to do a project like that." In fact, he says, "You meet people from all walks of life."

But Bob Sime had a personal reason for wanting to help. He tells us that when he was young, his father left his mother. So, his mother took him and his sister and moved in with another family.

"Back in those days you did that," he says. "Now, you don't have many places to go. It meant a lot to me to help somebody out, because we received help so long ago."

And as leaders of the project, John and Susan earned the respect of all those they've worked with over the years.

"We just love Susan and John," Roberta said. "They are such wonderful people."

Tim Berg adds, "The thing I think is interesting is getting a random phone call from Susan, and then you see all the work they're doing. You end up going to desserts and fundraisers, do the work, and then go out to dinner with them socially. It's interesting how things have developed from a phone call from a stranger 30 years ago to developing a friendship."

"John and Susan are just awesome," says Mike Young. "Their dedication and skill at fundraising and motivating people to get involved is absolutely amazing."

Sylvia Holden, who joined the Vision House team early in its tenure to help answer phones in the basement of the Camerer home, applauded Susan for her attention to detail and her willingness to roll up her sleeves to get things done. According to Sylvia, Susan developed a flower garden at her home, and one of her gifts to volunteers at the end of a job, on birthdays, or at garage sales, was a small bouquet of flowers.

"This was a high-impact and low-cost way to thank volunteers and people loved it," says Sylvia.

Diana Wallace reported that on many occasions when a handyman was needed to make light repairs or install a microwave or washing machine, Susan was the one to step up to do it.

"I saw her take on jobs that she'd never done before, but since there was no one else, she just rolled up her sleeves and struggled through."

And it's no surprise that John and Susan also earned a boatload of trust from these volunteers.

When asked what he would ask Vision House to do with an extra $150,000 if he had it to give, Jay Wallace said, "I'd give it to John and Susan to do whatever their biggest need was. I don't have any question as to the leadership. I completely trust them."

Jay said, "John and Susan just don't give up on people."

His wife, Diana, added, "It's not about them. They are so humble. It's about what God had going on, and they merely joined HIM."

IN CLOSING

For many, success is a fleeting fantasy. Something they only dream about. For others, it's a distant goal they spend their entire lives chasing.

For John and Susan Camerer, success was never in question, because they weren't looking for personal success. Frankly, they were too busy to care.

If it was success they were after, it was the individual successes of everyday people experiencing homelessness. Could this man fully recover from alcoholism? Could that mother find the courage to rise above her abuse? Could her children grow into happy healthy adults despite having lived on the street? Could they reunite as a family that would move into permanent housing?

What John and Susan were looking for each day was to finish one step of their arduous process before moving onto the next—to recruit one more volunteer, to raise one more dollar, to install one more bathroom or finish one more roof.

But finishing projects was never a question either, because their faith wasn't in themselves. Their faith was in God.

Throughout this entire process, the one constant in their lives was the belief that God was with them. They weren't looking for a Nobel Peace Prize. Nor were they looking for the adulation of the many people they met and worked with along the way.

But it's a funny thing about selfless acts of kindness. The people who perform them are focused only on the act itself and how it benefits someone else. They never focus on themselves.

But others do take note. Others will acknowledge the selflessness. And it is others who will applaud the effort.

This is the case at Vision House. There is an ongoing effort to care for and honor John and Susan as the Vision House founders—the young couple who gave it all in 1989 to create a program unparalleled in its work to minister to the homeless.

Melissa says it this way: "When I talk to donors, my job is to steward the work that John and Susan have created. I have been entrusted with this huge responsibility, and I seek to honor them and have staff recognize that as well."

From that Spring night when John and Susan watched the movie about the young mother and her daughter, to the decision to move forward with a program to help men experiencing homelessness, to taking on the enormous responsibility to build multi-story buildings to house families, to developing the kind of program that nurtures lost souls, Vision House has benefitted from their limitless belief in God, personal courage, and perseverance.

"It will always be important to honor what John and Susan have done for the homeless in our area," Melissa insists. "So, each year, we celebrate a Founders Day by choosing a local service project to accomplish for someone else."

Not only do staff and volunteers participate in this service project, the project is selected by John and Susan, and the couple work alongside the staff and volunteers as they do God's work for yet one more family who needs a helping hand.

And isn't that what you'd expect? For John and Susan to continue doing God's work?

John and Susan have left the ministry in capable hands, although it is never far from their thoughts or their hearts. They remain nearby in case they are needed for advice, counsel, or that annual service project.

Because what's one more good deed when you have a lifetime of good deeds behind you?

> *"His master replied, 'Well done, good and faithful servant!*
> *You have been faithful with a few things;*
> *I will put you in charge of many things.*
> *Come and share your master's happiness!'"*
> **—Matthew 25:23**

LIVES TRANSFORMED

We cannot share the stories of Vision House without highlighting a few of the families who have come, stayed, grown, and moved on to permanent housing of their own.

Names and some details may have been changed to protect their privacy.

Lisa

For most of us, the biggest obstacles in any given day are choosing what to wear or figuring out where to have lunch. But for others, their daily choices are much more consequential.

This was the case for Lisa.

Prior to coming to Vision House, Lisa's days were filled with the threat of domestic violence, sexual abuse, drug abuse, and rape—nothing close to normal.

She was completely unaware of what a healthy, loving relationship looked like. In fact, every woman in her family, dating back to her great grandmother, had been sexually violated in some manner. This left her without a positive role model for developing into an independent and healthy young woman.

Lisa married a man who was an alcoholic and drug abuser and extremely controlling. Her husband made all the decisions and kept her isolated and dependent on him. She was often raped during his drunken outbursts, and the emotional and physical violence against her became unbearable. She tried to leave on several occasions, but with three small children and an upbringing that strongly discouraged leaving her marriage, she remained trapped in a dangerous situation.

During his last violent outburst, her husband choked her to the point that she passed out. She thought she would surely die.

Lisa escaped and ran through the snow in her bare feet to the closest neighbor's home, which was miles away. She was forced to leave her three small girls behind, fearing they might not be alive when she returned.

Lisa and her daughters' lives were spared that horrific night. And with the help of authorities, she did finally leave her husband.

When Lisa arrived at Vision House, it was clear that she and her children had been through a great deal of trauma, and they displayed many of the symptoms consistent with PTSD. For instance, Lisa was hyper-vigilant with an exaggerated startle response. She suffered from anxiety and had a difficult time sleeping. And, she had what she called regular "PTSD attacks," or the feeling of impending fear that her husband was following her, would find her, and kill her and her children.

Lisa became diligent about pursuing the healing process and immersed herself in improving her mental health. With the help of her case manager, she set goals and found the appropriate physicians, counselors, domestic violence advocates, support groups, and other resources to help her find freedom from her internal bondage.

In the process, Lisa learned new life skills, such as managing her finances, budgeting, and positive parenting skills. She also learned ways to cope with her anxiety and how to reach out for help when needed. The experience at Vision House gave her new confidence, and someday, she says, she would like to use her experience to help other women who are enslaved by domestic violence.

Lastly, Lisa grew to know and trust God, seeing Him as a loving father who had her "in His hands," always wanting the very best for her and her children.

Janelle

Janelle says that her childhood was, "a life of getting beat up, shuffled around, and becoming homeless with my dad."

Her mom was on drugs, and to this day, has never admitted to her addiction or the consequences. She was reportedly mentally unstable, behaving in ways which were incredibly confusing for Janelle as a child.

Her mom left the family when Janelle was 11 years old, and her father hung out at the local bar, drinking all their money away. There was never enough food or decent clothes, and he regularly had strange women in and out of the house.

When they found themselves in a homeless situation, one of her father's old girlfriends took Janelle in so she wouldn't become a ward of the state. She says it was an awful place, where she was noticeably given less food, and the other children would be given new clothes while she was given hand-me-downs. Being raised in this manner, Janelle regularly felt deprived and unwanted.

This girlfriend stole all the money Janelle's grandmother had sent her, rendering Janelle financially helpless. The girlfriend also regularly used Janelle to go out and buy the street pills she needed to feed her addiction. She would then give pills to Janelle to keep her quiet. This was the beginning of Janelle's pill addiction and experience running drugs. She was only 13 years old.

At age 14, Janelle met a boy and moved in with him, having no other real safe place to be. Her childhood left her with few healthy coping skills and only an eighth-grade education. She eventually became involved in street crime to survive and found herself pregnant and with a baby at age 15.

Janelle was in and out of shelters until she was referred to Vision House. She and her daughter were accepted into the program, and she completed an outpatient chemical dependency treatment program as one of her first goals. Janelle had always struggled to finish what she started so completing her program was a big accomplishment. She remained sober throughout her stay and began a GED program at the local community college.

When asked how Vision House had helped her, Janelle replied, "I now finish things that I start, and I have learned to have higher standards for myself. I was lazy before, but I can do a lot more than I thought I could. I am less reactive, and I think things through more. And, I am more open to suggestions rather than doing things my own way."

Aisha

Aisha grew up in an unstable and chaotic home with alcoholic parents. Her parents divorced when she was six years old after her father left the family to begin a new life with a new wife and kids. This left Aisha feeling unloved, unworthy and abandoned. She and her brothers lived with their mother who was entrapped by her own addiction to alcohol and drugs, often having men in and out of the house and providing no comfort or stability for the children.

Aisha was 13 when she discovered that smoking pot and drinking provided some comfort from her internal confusion and pain. When she was 14 years old, Aisha witnessed her mother attempting to take her own life. This was a devastating experience and left her with significant emotional scars.

In the aftermath of this crisis, her father didn't want her, and she went to live with a childhood friend. This further deepened her feelings of anger, resentment, and abandonment. Neither of her parents were a source of support or comfort. She describes this time in her life as utterly chaotic.

At age 17, Aisha became aware that her life was beginning to go downhill as she continued to hide her pain behind the veil of drugs and alcohol.

Aisha married at age 20. The couple eventually bought a house, and she continued to drink in between her three pregnancies. She became addicted to pain medication after an injury, and the dual addiction to pills and alcohol began to overtake her life.

Her husband was active in his own addiction to alcohol, which eventually led to his job loss and then the loss of their home. They divorced, and Aisha was brought to her lowest point when she became homeless and lost temporary custody of her three precious girls.

Aisha spent 18 months in a substance abuse treatment program where she received counseling and spiritual guidance. This is where she heard about and applied to Vision House.

After a period of sobriety, Aisha and her three girls were accepted into the Vision House Family Program. When she first saw her new three-bedroom apartment, she was ecstatic because this was a chance at a new beginning.

While at Vision House, Aisha worked hard to understand where her life had gone wrong and learned to take responsibility for her mistakes. One thing she was clear about; she never wanted to be homeless again.

Vision House gave Aisha the time to attend counseling, develop a solid recovery program, address her parenting goals, and stabilize her children in the community and in school. She learned to prioritize, become financially self-sufficient, and budget her money. She attended church regularly and spent focused time reconnecting with the Lord, desperately wanting to lean on Him and give Him the glory for the doors He opened for her. She worked hard toward her educational goals and was able to complete a school certification program, which led to a new and exciting job that she now loves.

"I gained a lot of wisdom while I was there," she says. "I am so grateful to Vision House for everything they have done for us."

Through the grace of God, Aisha reunited with her ex-husband and they share a newfound commitment to their sobriety. Both now have full-time jobs and a new lease on life, and their family was able to move into a home, reaching their goal of permanent housing.

Ashley, Rachel and Cindy

Ashley, Rachel, and Cindy are sisters who benefitted from Vision House Shoreline. The two younger sisters came to the Community Center twice a week to partake in all the activities available to them. Not only was it good for them to socialize, they also spent time exploring their skills and interests.

The youngest, Cindy, is a very creative writer and often used the computer lab to write elaborate (and often hilarious) stories, which she would then read aloud to everyone's delight. Cindy was diagnosed with ADD later that year and struggled particularly in math. But Vision House helped her with her math, which also built her confidence.

The middle sister, Rachel, is a natural performer. She produced plays in the Community Center, always including all the children, and then performed them for the volunteers. She also worked with a tutor to improve her math skills.

Rachel and Cindy did their homework at the Community Center, where caring volunteers helped them, and they could earn prizes. The oldest sister, Ashley, is an artist and a musician. Vision House took them on a field trip to Seattle's Museum of Pop Culture, and Ashley spent hours in the music center, creating her own music with drums, guitar, and piano. She went on to receive the honor of Student of the Month for her excellence in art and has done multiple art projects at the Vision House Community Center.

When there was talk about moving into permanent housing, the girls clearly had mixed emotions. They wanted to live as a family in a place they could call their own, but they would miss the love and support they had while living at Vision House. Fortunately, they were able to heal as a family and grow as individuals, and with this new understanding, they were better prepared for the next chapter in their journey.

Patricia

Patricia had been conditioned to be afraid. She had experienced many forms of abuse and had become trapped in a vicious cycle, which eventually led to a man physically, mentally, and emotionally abusing her youngest daughter.

One day, her daughter asked her why she couldn't do anything about it. She told her that she was scared and didn't know how. So, they moved back in with her parents. And then, a devastating thing happened; she lost her mom to lung cancer. Her mom had been her rock and best friend and the only emotional support she had at that time. Patricia felt shattered.

She seriously considered suicide, until she took a long look at her kids; it was a huge wake-up call. She knew she needed help. A friend told her about Vision House. They were accepted into the program and went from sharing a bedroom and sleeping together on the floor to having their own rooms, a kitchen, and bathrooms.

"Seeing the apartment for the first time took my breath away," she says. "But my kids' reactions made me cry. They were thrilled." They all started counseling and Patricia started facing all the abuse in her life and realized that she truly was a survivor. She never wanted to be a victim again.

Vision House helped her find out who she really was. They helped her build a healthy new life. She says that God blessed them with Vision House.

"The greatest blessings have been having a roof over our heads, stability, security and a loving staff with knowledge and encouragement to keep me moving forward to become the person God intended me to be," Patricia says. "Without Vision House, I would have had to find a place to park my broken car so we could live out of it. I wouldn't have had the courage to face my fears, take on new challenges and start a new life. In fact, I just might have followed through on my thoughts of suicide. Because of Vision House I feel like a new person, seeing myself, for the first time, the way God sees me."

Note from the author

It was my honor to be asked to assemble and write this testimonial book commemorating the work Vision House has done since 1990 to transform the lives of men, women, and children experiencing homelessness. Although I am an author, I spent the better part of my life (over 35 years) as a nonprofit foundation executive, working on behalf of people who needed a helping hand. Whether it was to provide resources to solve a medical condition, to provide a peaceful haven for end-of-life care, to support children in all aspects of their growth, to champion the disabled, or to be a friend to shut-in seniors, I have seen first-hand the difference organizations like Vision House can make in our communities.

In my last role as executive director of the Renton Regional Community Foundation, I had the privilege of working with Vision House. So, it was an easy decision to accept this project, since I was already quite familiar with the quality and integrity of this outstanding organization. Now that I've retired, while I continue to author books, I have chosen to work largely on behalf of the nonprofit community, helping organizations all over the world be all they can be through better messaging and communications.

Lastly, I'd like to say a few words about John and Susan Camerer. I have known them for many years and have the highest regard for them, both personally and professionally. It is not often you find people who are willing to sacrifice so much for the benefit of others. And yet, they will shrug off any attempt at lauding their efforts. They will always give the credit for making a difference to their faith in God.

But I am someone who recognizes that an individual's faith doesn't always translate into tangible results, at least not at this level. That takes more than faith. It takes guts. And, in my opinion, John and Susan are champions of the highest caliber regardless of their religious beliefs. To the core, these are good and true people who deserve our thanks and appreciation for making this world a better place.

I have often said that if there was a good-deed-o-meter in heaven, we should each be aware of the score we accumulate in our daily lives. Have we done too little? Have we done enough? In the end, we should always strive to do more than enough. We should do enough to ring that bell at the top of the meter so loudly that even God's ears might ring. Just the way John and Susan Camerer have done countless times.

If you'd like more information on my books or my freelance writing services, please visit me online at: LilDogCommunications.com or *LynnBohart-author.com*

~*Lynn Bohart*

Become a Vision House champion

Vision House was born out of a God-given conviction in the hearts of John and Susan Camerer to support single moms with kids at risk of ending up on the streets. They have provided transitional housing and supportive services since 1990 to help families in crisis move to stability and self-sufficiency.

Vision House serves custodial parents with children, including single mothers, single fathers, and two-parent families. Their program is infused with a deep commitment and passion to see lives changed and to see the cycle of homelessness broken for the next generation.

To learn more about Vision House, please visit **VisionHouse.org**. There you will find information about their programs, as well as how you can get involved:

- Volunteer opportunities
- Thrift store and donation guidelines
- Financial donation opportunities
- Employment opportunities
- Upcoming events
- ....and more

While Vision House is a faith-based organization, it serves and welcomes all and does not discriminate.

Vision House reaffirms its policy of non-discrimination on the basis of minority status, gender, creed, religious or other impermissible grounds in the provision of all services to eligible members of the public.

Vision House commits itself to a continuing program to assure that unlawful discrimination does not occur in the service it renders to the public.

[i] "Behind Closed Doors: The Impact of Domestic Violence on Children." UNICEF, Child Protection Section and The Body Shop International (2006).

[ii] Strauss, Gelles, and Smith, "Physical Violence in American Families: Risk Factors and Adaptations to Violence" in 8,145 Families. Transaction Publishers (1990).

[iii] Volpe, J.S., "Effects of Domestic Violence on Children and Adolescents: An Overview", The American Academy of Experts in Traumatic Stress, 1996.

DomesticShelters.org